Jumi
Abbe

Jacques Le Maho
Research Director, CNRS

Within the majestic setting of a meander in the Seine, the abbatial towers emerging from the tree tops always make a strong impression on visitors discovering Jumièges peninsula. Once the porch of the Church of Notre-Dame has been traversed, it is then the striking vision of its façade, in all its power and austere majesty, which grips us. The mysterious atmosphere emanating from the locale, the mutilated architectural splendours, and the serenity of parks and shaded pathways seduce amateurs of romantic promenades as well.

Jumièges is also a major historic and archaeological site. Founded by Saint Philibert in the 7th century, the abbey was one of the very first monastic residences in the lower Seine valley. Abandoned during the 9th-century Viking raids, it was rebuilt from around 940, before becoming one of the great centres of the Norman religious and cultural renaissance. Constructed between 1040 and 1067, the Church of Notre-Dame numbers amongst the principal building works from the start of William the Conqueror's reign. Lastly, within the entry of the Church of Saint-Pierre, Jumièges conceals elevations from the high Middle Ages. According to recent analyses, antecedent to the Viking period, they date amongst the very rarest Carolingian architectural traces to survive north of the Loire.

Veue
DE IV
de L'ordre de
gation de St.
Rouen, dans
logis abbatial

'Abbaye.
EGES.
enoist. Congre=
r ; à 5. lieües de
is de Caux 1702.

654
The foundation

Preceding double page **Jumièges Abbey in 1702,** watercolour from the Collection Gaignières (Paris, BnF).

Originally from Éauze in the Gers region, Philibert received his education within the court of King Dagobert I († 639). At age seventeen, he entered the monastery at Rebais, where he became abbot. But his craving for asceticism drove him to depart and install himself in Luxeuil in the Vosges, then in Bobbio in Italy. In 654, having returned to Gaul, he founded Jumièges monastery where, from its inception, he instituted the rule of Saint Benedict, which the majority of Norman abbeys were to follow.

Queen Bathilde's tunic, 7th century (Chelles, Musée municipal).

Discovered intact in a reliquary, it is ornamented with jewel-studded embroidery, donated to the poor by the Queen upon her retirement to Chelles monastery in 664.

Queen Bathilde

In his undertaking, Philibert was assisted by Queen Bathilde († 680). Of Anglo-Saxon descent, Bathilde was a former slave, sent to Gaul to serve Erchinoald, mayor of the Palace♦ of Neustria. Since the death of Clovis, Frankish Gaul had effectively been divided into two kingdoms: Neustria to the northwest and Austrasia. Bathilde attracted the attention of King Clovis II, who took her for his wife. Having become queen, she devoted herself unstintingly to charitable works, founding the monasteries at Chelles (Seine-et-Marne region) and Corbie (Somme region), and aiding numerous religious establishments with donations of land and funds. To Philibert, she ceded the Jumièges estate, a vast royal property situated in a meander of the Seine, with fishing rights in the river and diverse forestry outbuildings. Such proximity of royal power ceased to be an advantage at the end of the Merovingian epoch, during instances of rivalry between the aristocracy and mayors of the Palace.

Under Philibert's administration

Philibert built four churches in his monastery, the principal one dedicated to Saint Peter, the other three to the Virgin Mary, Saint Denys, and Saint Germanus. No historical traces have been retained on his admin-

♦Mayor of the palace: *first dignitary, after the king, in the Merovingian court.*

istrative role at Jumièges, apart from the development of business relations with England, to which he became attached. According to his anonymous biographer, the abbot of Jumièges had given an order to his merchants (likely based upon a notion of Queen Bathilde, who had not forgotten her origins): to sell merchandise at a high price and to use the profits to buy up slaves who were to be brought back free to Jumièges. New members joined the monastery, attracted by its renown, and the number of monks rapidly grew considerable. To the men's abbey at Jumièges, Philibert annexed a monastery for women, first installed on a property of Duke Amalbert (perhaps Notre-Dame-de-Bondeville), then transferred to Pavilly and placed under the direction of Austreberthe, abbess of Port-le-Grand, near Abbeville.

Jumièges Abbey deniers, end of the 7th century (Paris, BnF). These coins are amongst the rare known evidence of Merovingian currency of the Rouen diocese abbeys.

Implicated in a conflict over succession at the death of Clotaire III, Bathilde's son, Philibert was denounced by partisans of the mayor of Ebroïn Palace and incarcerated on orders from Saint Ouen, Bishop of Rouen. Once liberated, he left Jumièges, offered his services to Bishop Ansoald of Poitiers, and founded the monastery at Hério on the Île de Noirmoutier. Reconciled with Saint Ouen, he returned to Jumièges in 683, building a new establishment for women at Montivilliers. He died in 685 at the Noirmoutier monastery, where he is buried. From that moment, he would be counted among the saints.

Abbot Hugues

The last great abbot of Jumièges during the Merovingian period was Hugues († circa 733), also Abbot of Fontenelle (Saint-Wandrille region), Bishop of Bayeux and of Paris. Indicative of his preference for Jumièges, it was here that he wished to establish his sepulchre, in the Church of Notre-Dame. At the beginning of the 9th century, his tomb was still exhibited there, covered with a baldaquin ornamented by precious metals.

Merovingian column and capital, Jumièges, marble. Reused in the Church of Duclair, they doubtless came from Notre-Dame's nave, placed between 942 and 945.

8th and 9th centuries
Carolingian period

At the Church of Saint-Pierre at Jumièges that, by the grace of God, is directed by the Abbot Héribert.

Act of Pépin, King of Aquitaine, 838.

A precious description of the Carolingian-period abbey is contained in the *Vie de saint Philiber*t [The Life of Saint Philibert], written from the 8th to 9th century: "A square enclosure bristling with towers, some sumptuous reception halls endowed with all that is necessary to welcome visitors. Within, the domestic premises are nothing but splendid, comfortable, and dignified. At sunrise looms up a cruxiform church dominated by an image of the sweet Virgin Mary; it contains an altar to Saint Philibert [...] resplendent in precious stones, gold and silver, and to the sides, some altars in honour of Saint John and Saint Columbanus. On the north side are two chapels honouring Saint Denys and Saint Germanus. To the right is the noble Church [of] Saint-Pierre with the Saint-Martin chapel to one side. At noon Saint Philibert's cell is shown, with its splendid stone balustrade [...]. To the south rises a building 280 feet long by 50 wide; this is the dormitory. Each bed is illuminated by a paned window, permitting everyone to read by daylight. The ground floor is occupied by two pantries, one used as a larder, the other as a kitchen [...]."

With the exception of the west portion of Saint-Pierre—perhaps slightly posterior to the compilation of this text—none of these edifices survived. But, as reconstructions went on, the general disposition of the site remained unchanged: the gateway to the west, a large building housing the refectory, the kitchen and dormitory on the southern side, and a small basement on the presumed location of Saint Philibert's cell to the south-east of Saint-Pierre.

Jumièges is one of those Norman abbeys where continuity of the Carolingian plan remains clearly perceptible today. Thus, for the first time, a text, the *Vie de saint Philibert*, testifies to characteristics of future Norman abbeys: their impressive dimensions, multiplicity of churches, and sumptuous furnishings which made the Vikings covet them deeply.

Tassilon of Bavaria's chalice,
late 8th century (Kremsmünster Treasure-house, Austria).
For having broken his pledge of allegiance to Charlemagne, Duke Tassilon of Bavaria was put on trial in Ingelheim in June 788 and condemned to exile. According to 10th-century tradition, he was interned at Jumièges with his son Theodon.

8 | **Saint-Riquier: sister-abbey to Jumièges** (Somme), print, 1612 (Paris, BnF). At either end of the nave, a transept is surmounted by a tower. The churches of Notre-Dame and Saint-Pierre of Jumièges must have presented an analogous layout.

Norman invasions

In the month of May 841, a flotilla commanded by the Danish chief Ragnar sailed up the Seine to Rouen. The city was pillaged during two days. In descending the river, the Vikings stopped at Jumièges, sacking the abbey and setting its buildings on fire. The abbey never recovered from this first raid.

From the mid-9th century, Viking flotilla processions along the Seine became incessant. In 862, a Scandinavian army which had evacuated the camp at Jeufosse, near Mantes, made a stopover at the port of Jumièges to repair ships before setting out to sea. It soon became impossible for the monks to eke out a living on the site. Before 885, they were forced to withdraw to Haspres in the Cambrai region.

Norman warships, Bayeux tapestry, 9th century, detail (Bayeux, Centre Guillaume-le Conquérant).

The baptism of Rollo terminates Norman invasions, miniature from the *Chroniques de France*, 14th century (Paris, BnF).

From the Pact of Jumièges to the Treaty of Saint-Clair-sur-Epte

The chronicler Dudon de Saint-Quentin reported as follows an encounter which is believed to have taken place toward the end of the 9th century at Jumièges between the Viking chief Rollo and some emissaries of the Archbishop of Rouen: "Once they learned that a strong Norman contingent was positioned at Jumièges, the local inhabitants (many of whom were merchants ruined by the war and others without resources) left the matter in the hands of Françon, Archbishop of Rouen. The latter sent an ambassador to Rollo to propose a pact. Seeing that the city of Rouen and its region were inhabited solely by a population without defences, Rollo made a promise not to attack them."

This interview prefigures that of Saint-Clair-sur-Epte (911), during the course of which was concluded an accord stipulating that Rollo could have the city of Rouen and its surrounding lands at his disposal. This act acknowledged the invaders' possession of what was to become Normandy. Their settlement put an end to the havoc. Rollo was baptised in 912 and became the first duke of Normandy. Having converted, the Norman dukes favoured the rebirth of abbeys destroyed during Viking raids.

10th century
A renaissance

At the outset of the 10th century, the monks who had sought refuge in the Cambrai sent two of their members, Gandoin and Baudoin, back to Jumièges to repossess the site. Their first task consisted of uprooting bushes and brambles that had invaded the buildings. Around 940, the Duke of Normandy, Guillaume Longue-Épée (son of Rollo), decided to rebuild the abbey. He had the Carolingian Church of Saint-Pierre placed away from the water, refitted a section of the old monastic buildings, and confined the monastery to Martin, abbot of Saint-Cyprien of Poitiers, who arrived accompanied by twelve monks. The Duke assured them a minimum of resources by restituting several former properties to the abbey.

Right page
Manuscript of Saint Augustin (detail of an illuminated letter), the oldest evidence of the Norman art of illumination, 10th century (Rouen, BM). Jumièges, painted manuscript production was of major importance to the history of the cultural renaissance of the country in the 10th century.

In 942, for reasons of territorial rivalry, the assassination of Guillaume Longue-Épée sharply halted this renaissance. For three years, Rouen lived under the control of King Louis IV, who favoured the abbey of Saint-Ouen over the dependencies of Jumièges and ordered the destruction of the Church of Notre Dame's vestiges. Only the stout towers situated at the two extremities of the nave were saved, bought up by a cleric named Clément. The abbey was thus in great danger of disappearing yet again. As self-defence against French propaganda from the last Carolingian kings, the monks composed several texts destined to highlight Jumièges' history (*Vie de Saint Aycadre* and *Vie de Saint Hugues*) and to celebrate the memory of the departed Duke, notably in the *Complainte sur la mort de Guillaume Longue-Épée* [Lament Over the Death of Guillaume Longue-Épée], the most ancient hymn in Norman history. In this text, Guillaume is presented as a highly Christian prince (who himself had momentarily dreamed of becoming a monk at Jumièges) and as a peace-loving ruling defender of orphans and the poor.

Silver denier of Guillaume Longue-Épée, recto and verso, circa 927-942 (Rouen, MDSM). Guillaume Longue-Épée was the first Duke of Normandy to strike coins in his name.

STS PETRUS
uox
fide
uerbera · flagella · carcer
generatormentor
nuit · ut omis pie uiuentes

Saint Anselme seated between two monks. Illuminated letter from a Jumièges manuscript, attributed to the painter identified with the signature "Hugo Pictor". (Rouen, BM).

A Benedictine abbey

Not a single document sheds light on the extent of monastery members before the 9th-century Norman invasions. In the 13th century, there numbered about fifty friars, with a maximum of fifty-seven by around mid-century. In 1562, there were only seventeen. The numbers then increased, primarily due to an influx of new recruits attracted to the reforms. Yet on the eve of the Revolution, they again numbered fewer than twenty.

At the head of the community was the abbot, both temporal and spiritual head of the establishment. Next in hierarchy came the prior and several sub-priors charged with training, supervision, and discipline of the monks, as well as instruction of the novices. Management of different church duties at the abbey (the "offices") was handed down to the friars, chosen according to their particular competences: the cantor, master of the chapel, and master of ceremonies; the sacristy (sexton); the storehouse keeper, charged with provisions and communal stores for wine and food; the refectioner and cook; the nurse; the chaplain, responsible for welcoming pilgrims and the poor at the monastery's gate; and the treasurer, in charge of finances. Certain duties were reserved for the laity who resided apart from the cloister, such as the provost (or bailiff), charged with worldly administration and the law. The abbey equally housed a full staff: domestics, tailors, cobblers, laundresses, kitchen aids, butchers, bakers, gardeners, cowherds, ostlers, and wardens. A document dated 1413 estimated the number of servants lodged within the outbuildings at thirty-two.

Daily life

Throughout the entire day, chiming bells were heard calling the monks to prayer: the largest bells were situated in the tower over the crossing at the Church of Notre-Dame, but there were others atop the summit of the façade turrets and on the gable of the chapter-house hall. Numerous church services followed sequentially within brief intervals, from vigils (in the middle of the night) until vespers and complins. It seems that night services were for a long while celebrated in the Church of Saint-Pierre, close to the dormitory. Others took place in the abbatial Church of Notre-Dame, where the monks had their stalls, on the floor of the transept. There the abbot maintained a special seat at his disposal, but he officiated only during formal ceremonies and enjoyed an individual chapel adjoined to his apartments. Celebrations honouring the saints of Jumièges and important dates in the liturgical cycle led to special formalities, and to complex, meticulously orchestrated ceremonials. Often they were accompanied by processions from chapel to chapel, traversing cloister galleries, or from one part of the monastery buildings to another.

To the rhythm of prayers

A number of events and quotidian acts—now considered banal—had to be accompanied by the recitation of a short prayer meant to recall that, in the monastery enclosure, all places, gestures, and words assumed a sacred character. Liturgical manuals written at Jumièges during the 11th and 12th centuries have preserved formulas for prayers to pronounce for every conceivable circumstance: when brothers entered or left the kitchen; when they departed on a voyage or returned; welcoming a foreign brother to the abbey; the benediction of a reader at the refectory; the blessing of water and common places; the blessing of food; prayers to recite before and after meals; benediction over fresh bread, fruits, wine, produce of the vineyards; the prayer to recite against lightning; blessing over the wardrobe, library, farmyard, grange, bakehouse, wells, butcher shop or warming room. Each day, summoned by the bells, the monks assembled in the chapter house where a chapter, or capitulum, from the rule of Saint-Benedict was read. It was also in this location that the friars debated administrative questions, discipline problems, and all else that touched upon the life of the monastery.

Between two church services, the cloister galleries or garden pathways offered the monks a place to rest, promenade, or read. In winter, they gathered around the fireplace in the warming room. If, initially, monks participated in work in the fields—in a 9th-century illuminated manuscript, one observes monks harvesting manually—later, their manual tasks were limited essentially to copy work: from all parts, the abbey borrowed books which were given to its most able calligraphers to transcribe.

Evangelistary collect, genaeology according to Saint Luke, 12th-13th century (Rouen, BM).

Liturgical bassin within one of the chapels in Notre-Dame's choir, 13th century.

From the 11th to the 14th century

A second renaissance

Year 1040, the foundations of the Church of Notre-Dame were laid by the Abbot Robert.

Jumièges Annals, 12th century.

Jumièges' abbatial "Tau", walrus-tusk ivory, end of the 11th century (Rouen, Musée départemental des Antiquités). As a sign of their function, 11th-century abbots used a cane furnished with an ivory handle, called a "tau" because of its T-shape.

Sixteen years after Guillaume de Volpiano's arrival at Fécamp in 1001, as the great propagator of Benedictine rule, one of his disciples, Thierry, a monk from Saint-Bénigne in Dijon, was called on to direct Jumièges Abbey. He ensured strict observation of the rule, obtained a charter of confirmation of abbatial properties from Duke Richard II in 1025, and undertook major building works. He had the Church of Notre-Dame's old west tower restored and there refurbished a chapel, consecrated on 18 March and dedicated to the Savior (Saint Sauveur).

When in 1037 Robert Champart was named Abbot of Jumièges, the ancient Church of Notre-Dame was still split into two parts, each having at its nucleus one of the stout towers which had escaped 10th-century demolitions: Saint-

An historian of 11th-century Normandy

Guillaume Caillou, a Jumièges monk, compiled the work *Histoire des ducs de Normandie* between 1066 and 1072, dedicated to William the Conqueror. Following upon the chronicle of Dudon de Saint-Quentin, who was arrested during the reign of Richard I († 996), this work constitutes a fundamental source for the history of the duchy between year 1000 and the beginning of the 1070s. Already celebrated in its day, it was used by successive generations of Norman chroniclers, from Guillaume de Poitiers (circa 1074) to Robert de Torigni (mid-12th century).

Guillaume of Jumièges presenting his book to William the Conqueror, 12th century (Rouen, BM).

Robert Champart, Abbot of Jumièges, became bishop of London in 1045. He offered Jumièges a sacramentary (below, Rouen, BM), which inspired sculptors of the Church of **Notre-Dame,** then under construction (centre, Laurent Renou model, 1986). This church no doubt served as model for **Westminster Abbey Church,** represented in this scene from the Bayeux tapestry (top, Bayeux, Centre Guillaume-le-Conquérant).

Sauveur chapel to the extreme west, and Notre-Dame chapel to the extreme east. Abbot Robert undertook their reconstruction and restoration to their original unified state. Such was the origin of the grand Church of Notre-Dame, whose traces are still visible. The first construction stone was laid in 1040. Starting with the chevet, work was directed from east to west. The choir was likely completed when Abbot Robert died in 1055: it is here, near the main altar, that he was buried. On 1 July 1067, a "dedication" at last marked the completion of the edifice and its official opening to worship. Presided over by Maurille, Archbishop of Rouen, this ceremony took place in the presence of William the Conqueror. Less than a year after his victory at the Battle of Hastings (which placed him on the throne of England), William was at the height of his glory. Those present also included the Bishops of Coutances, Avranches, Lisieux, and Evreux, along with a crowd of barons.

Illuminated manuscripts

Breviary, Christmas service, 12th century (Rouen, BM).

After a sharp decline in manuscript production in the last decades of the 10th century, the arrival of Thierry (disciple of the great reformer Guillaume de Volpiano) at Jumièges in 1017 marked the beginning of an intellectual renaissance at the abbey. A number of volumes were then transcribed to enrich the library, permitting the teaching of the Holy Scriptures and furnishing support for the liturgy. Religious works were generally embellished with linear or painted illumination. Especially active by the mid-11th century, the Jumièges workshop has left us with a great quantity of these illuminated manuscripts, characterised by the employment of reddish-orange ink drawings.

The Jumièges Bible, 11th century

This is a major work with respect to the illuminated manuscripts done by Norman monks and gives profound new insight into contemporary conceptions on the subject of illuminated lettering. Gifted with a rare decorative imagination, the artist intermingles plant-inspired elements such as stems or small branches; animals, and characters in an astonishing variety of compositions. This bible is believed to have been executed at the start of Gontard's abbacy (1078-1095).

Opposite and right page **Jumièges bible,** 11th century (Rouen, BM).

"I transcribed this work during freezing weather: reader, be forgiving." *Annotation in a Jumièges manuscript, 12th century*

The Life of Saint Aycadre, last quarter of the 11th century

Under a triple-arcaded portico is a scene of three figures. Centrally seated is Saint Aycadre, fourth Abbot of Jumièges († circa 693), in one hand upholding a palm and, with the other, handing back a crozier (a sign of abbatial dignity) to a friar (placed to his left), perhaps the abbot upon whose orders was written the life of the saint. To his left, another monk presents him with an open book, undoubtedly itself the work in question. This masterfully accomplished drawing was probably executed by the artist who illustrated the Jumièges bible.

The Life of Saint Aycadre, last quarter of the 11th century (Rouen, BM).

uctra

Nolite

.Adhuc

terra.

tes. a

mplebo

um. e

uum.

plus

nloco

ucessi-

to dam

am

rpa

N

S

d

ac

su

ac

ue

in

ciru

clam

hec

mun

nh

A rich and prosperous abbey

Beginning with the first core of properties inherited from the pre-Norman period, donations given to the monastery, almost continually in flux until the late 12th century, ended up constituting a rich heritage which extended over a vast region around the lower Seine.

These settlements were most often derived from seigneurs desirous to purchase spiritual peace of mind. Donations were extremely varied in nature: a church, mills, lands, rents, tithes, and even entire estates, including persons who lived there. The main unity of exploitation was the "grange", the equivalent of a large farm, endowed with vast living quarters and an entire complex of buildings. In their compendium of property titles, the Jumièges monks noted with great care the

Bushel- standard made in 1570 for the Jumièges monks; this grain measure was utilised by the tax collector of the baronny of Duclair (Rouen, Musée départemental des Antiquités)

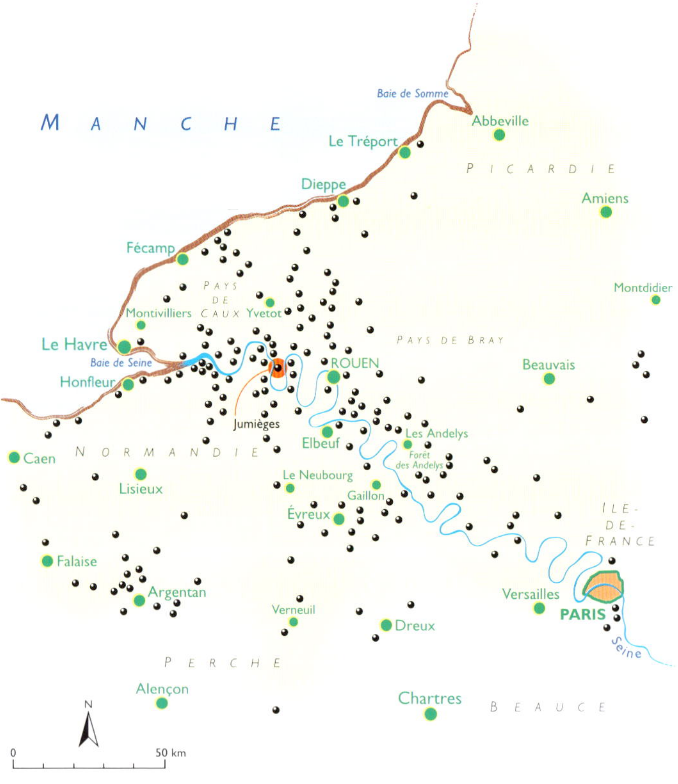

Map of abbey possessions
in Upper Normandy and bordering regions in the late Middle Ages.

Ruins of Cour-du-Mont manor at Duclair (Seine-Maritime). Double portal in a 12th-century gable wall. This manor was one of the abbey "granges" on the right bank of the Seine.

Heurteauville grange (Seine-Maritime), 13th century. Vestige of an important abbey property on the left bank of the Seine.

nature of annual rental charges, owed by the peasants, collected from their estates. The abbey was equally paid rights to numerous markets installed in the towns and in Jumièges itself. During a period of economic prosperity enjoyed by Normandy from the 11th to the 15th century, the establishment benefited from steady resources, often excessive in relation to current needs of various "offices", or church services of the abbey. A large part of the surplus was reinvested in building work: the abbey became a quasi-permanent construction site from the early 11th century to the first decades of the 14th century. The splendiferous buildings surviving on the site are without doubt the most eloquent testimony of Jumièges' financial strength in the Middle Ages.

Hauville windmill (Eure), 13th century. This mill (restored in 1984) was constructed for the Jumièges monks, proprietors of the rich Hauville estate on the Roumois plateau.

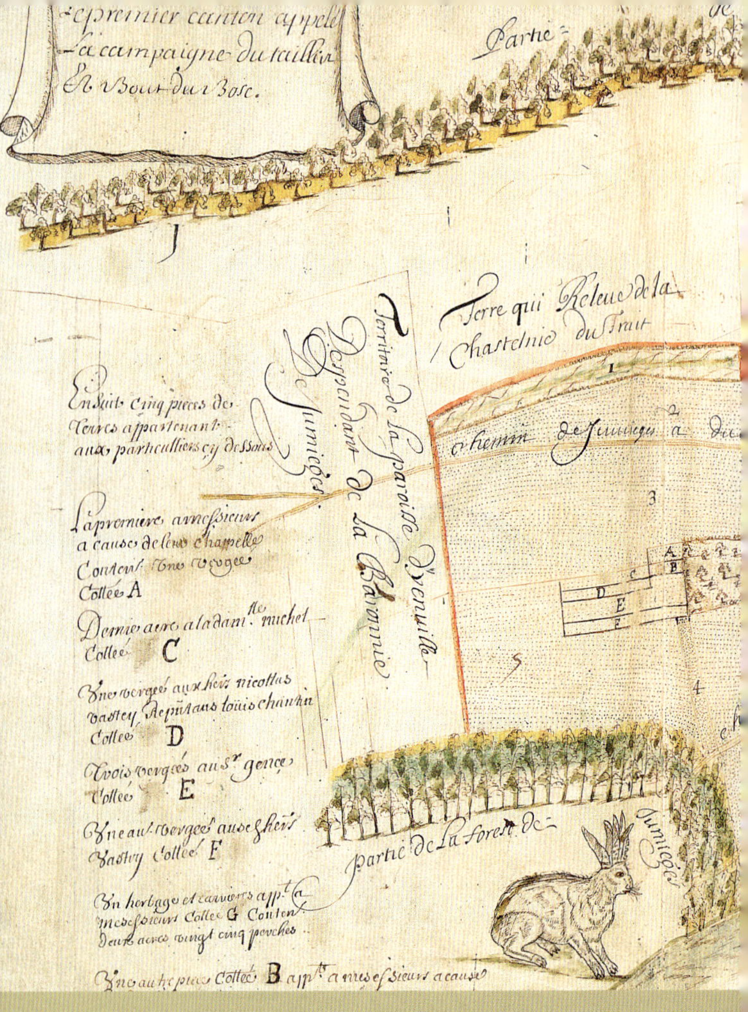

"The Seine, renown for its commercial vessels and its abundant fish." *Chronique de Saint-Wandrille*, beginning of the 9th century.

The abbey and the Seine

"From all angles, this celebrated site is surrounded by water [...]. The Seine there describes a curve of three nautical miles, and lazily advances the five, even eight arms which make up its course. Only one of these arms is capable of serving navigation. Sometimes, in rising, the sea spews forth there, sometimes it stops and returns to its bed [...]. What is most extraordinary—and that one never has by hearsay—is the advantage it brings in capturing sea monsters; with some harpoons, nets, and in boats one hauls in ones that are fifty feet long. Their flesh nourishes the brothers, the oil of their fat chases away the gloom. An astonishing thing! The water, which naturally extinguishes fire, here procures the fat which feeds the lamp flame." It was in these enthusiastic terms at the beginning of the 9th century, in his introduction to the *Vie de saint Philibert* that the monk Ermentaire described the site of Jumièges and the riches of the river, an inexhaustible source of benefits for the brothers. Hunting for cetaceans, then plentiful in the bay of the Seine, was one of their fishing fleets' specialities during the Carolingian period.

On the eve of the Revolution, fishing still represented one of the principal resources of the Jumièges peninsula: "Fishing took the place of a fortune for a sector of these people [of the peninsula] who are never employed there in futile: today one still catches sturgeon, salmon, shad, pike, carp, and smelt, each in their season, besides a prodigious quantity of little fish that individuals buy and on which fishermen themselves live" (Dom Dubusc, *Histoire de l'abbaye*

The Seine at Duclair, watercolour plan, 17th century (Rouen, ADSM). Different types of boats are here illustrated: merchant ships, small fishing vessels with sharply raised prows.

royale de Saint-Pierre de Jumièges [History of the royal abbey of Saint-Pierre of Jumièges]. From the 7th century, Queen Bathilde had accorded the brothers the right to exploit the waters of the meander, which assured them one of their main resources, river fishing. The abbey also controlled several water passages, for which it collected tolls, as well as ports, of which the most important was that of Quillebeuf, an obligatory stopover for ships going up the Seine toward Rouen. The monks owned their own boats—a liturgical manual of the abbey contains a special prayer formula for the "benediction of a new ship"—but, as a general rule, fishermen and boatsmen of the peninsula exercised their trade in an independent manner. They were subjected only to licence fee payments in kind or in silver. Settlement was made on a fixed date, according to a ritual which kept a certain solemnity in the 16th and 17th centuries. Upon convocation by an officer of the abbey, each vassal holding a right to fishing was obliged to present himself annually to the monastery, to proceed thrice round the dovecote tower (symbol of seigneurial rights of the abbey), after which each one knocked at the door, offered salutations, paid five *sous* for annual net casting, and took leave.

Frontal cranium of a whale found in the navigation channel, Jumièges (Rouen, Muséum d'histoire naturelle).

From the 14th to the 17th century
Wars and reforms

The Hundred Years' War (1337-1450)

Charles VII by Jean Fouquet (Paris, Musée du Louvre).

The abbey had not yet suffered enormously from hostilities when, in 1358, it was invaded by a troop of eight hundred men in the pay of Charles the Bad, King of Navarre. To avoid its becoming once again a haunt of armed bands, the Regent Charles (son of King John the Good, then in captivity) had the tower staircases destroyed in August 1359.

After 1415, the region submitted to English occupation; to protect Jumièges, Abbot Nicolas le Roux was forced to take an oath of loyalty to Henry V. A peasant insurrection obliged the monks to evacuate the new abbey in 1434. When the country was finally liberated, in 1450, the financial situation was terribly worrying. Concerning the buildings, reparations were limited to absolute essentials, starting with reinstating kitchens and service premises.

During the liberation campaign at the beginning of 1450, Charles VII installed himself for five weeks at Jumièges. The king was accompanied by his mistress, Agnès Sorel, lodged in the La Vigne manor at Mesnil-sous-Jumièges, which was abbey property.

There, after having given birth to a girl, she passed away on 9 February 1450. Her heart was deposed in the Church of Notre-Dame's north transept chapel.

Recumbent figure of an abbot, 15th century (Collection de l'abbaye). Sometimes considered to be Simon du Bosc († 1418). He played a notable role during the Great Schism which divided Christianity and lived to succeed two popes.

Right page
Agnès Sorel, painting attributed to Jean Clouet, (Château de Loches, Indre-et-Loire).

Period of reforms

In 1464, the abbey passed through the commendam system: it was nevertheless placed under the direction of abbots named by the king and benefited from the usufruct of abbatial revenues, without residential obligation. A relaxation of the rule followed. During the 16th century, there was a desire to reform the establishment. In 1516, Abbot Philippe de Luxembourg brought twenty friars from Chézal-Benoît♦, near Issoudun (Cher region), but despite the official unification of the abbey with this congregation in 1526, the Chézal-Benoît reform would never really be applied there. In November 1616, Dom Langlois, former prior, requested Jumièges' affiliation with the Saint-Vanne congregation. From the latter, two years later, the Saint-Maur congregation♦ was dispatched. Jumièges had thus become one of the finest jewels, housing the province of Normandy's novitiate. Institution of commendam rule and establishment of reforms were not without repercussions on the buildings. Rather than assuming costs to maintain the spire of Notre-Dame's large tower, Abbot Gabriel Le Veneur had it demolished in 1557 in order to resell its lead. When, in the 16th century, the first reform monks arrived at Jumièges, a separate dormitory was constructed for them, on the south side of the Church of Saint-Pierre. In the next century, the introduction of the Saint Maurus reform necessitated a sharing out of the abbey between newcomers and the so-called "elder" monks, who refused any change to their status. To the Maurists went the Church of Notre-Dame and the principal monastic structures; to the Elders, the Church of Saint-Pierre and, amongst the outbuildings, all those structures susceptible to transformation into individual dwellings. Between 1607 and 1613, the Abbot of Martimbos had himself built a dwelling in the park.

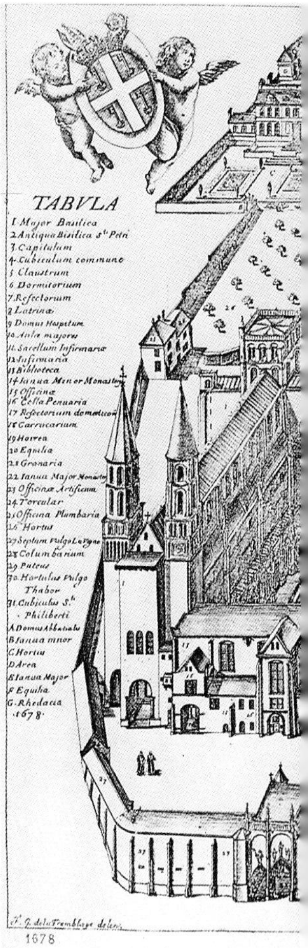

1678

♦ ***Chézal-Benoît (Cher):*** *headquarters of a congregation of Benedictine monasteries founded in 1488. It united with the congregation of Saint-Maur in 1636.*

♦ ***Congregation of Saint-Maur:*** *Benedictine congregation founded in Paris in 1618 and dissolved during the Revolution, it had a strong intellectual and spiritual influence.*

Report of great turmoil

Like so many other abbeys, Jumièges suffered during the Religious Wars. In 1562, a Huguenot raid forced the monks to take refuge in Rouen. They hid the treasury in the abbatial courtyard, but could not prevent the pillage of a large portion of ornaments; loss was estimated at more than 15,000 livres, a considerable sum. Between October 1591 and April 1592, battles during the Wars of the League drove hordes of unfortunates onto the roads.
A number of them found asylum in the abbey: "The kings' apartment, dormitories, infirmaries, the abbatial dwelling, hostelry, and even the garrets

The abbey in 1678, seen from the west, engraved plate from *Monasticon Gallicanum.*

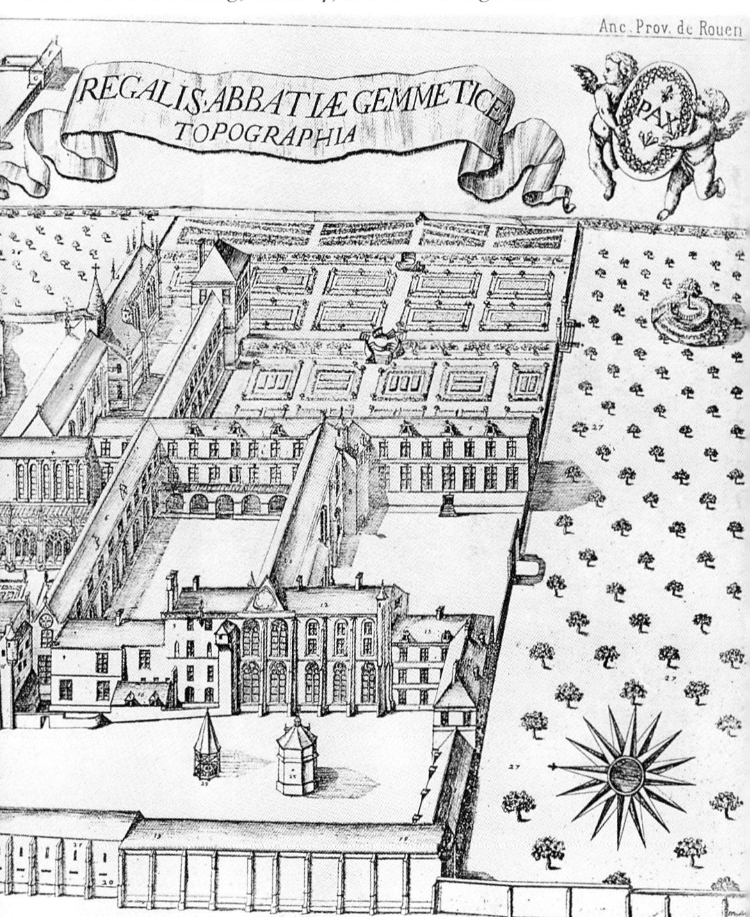

were filled up. There were entire households in the refectory, bakery, laundry, press-house, and bell tower" (Dom Dubusc).
Much later, during the troubles of the Fronde, which marked Louis XIV's minority (between 1648 and 1652), the monks had to face a renewed influx of refugees.

17th and 18th centuries
Architectural work of the Maurists

Staircase in the park constructed by the Maurists.

Right page **Abbatial dwelling interior.**

♦ ***Maurist:*** *brother in the Saint-Maur congregation.*

Abbey seen from the Seine, 17th-century print (Paris, BnF).

After the 1660s, with the last Elders having disappeared and their properties reunited with those of the community, the Maurists♦ were in a position to buckle down to large construction projects. In 1665, they raised the larder wing to the west of the cloister to establish a vast library there, symbol of an intellectual revival at the abbey.

Between 1665 and 1671, Abbot François de Harlay de Champvallon, Archbishop of Paris, built a new abbatial dwelling. Constructed at a distance from the abbey within the north-east sector of the park, this edifice survives today more or less as it existed originally.

In the prolongation of the cloisters' east wing between 1701 and 1732, the Maurists embarked on erecting a costly new dormitory comprised of vestibules and reception halls on the ground floor, and forty-nine cells on the first floor. Together with two lateral pavilions, the ensemble extended over more than 80 metres in length. On the eve of the Revolution, only minor modifications were introduced there: transfer of the hostelry and infirmary to the ground floor in 1772-1773, and installation of an ornamental pediment on the façade in 1777.

1789-1918
Destruction and rediscovery

Do not destroy them, these pious edifices,
Where courage has just healed their old scars.
Léon Halévy, 1837, Jumièges golden book

Right page
Shepherd wandering through cloister ruins, detail of Alexandre Évariste Fragonard's illustration for Taylor and Nodier's *Voyages pittoresques ...*, 1820 (Paris, BnF).

On 13 April 1790, when the Revolutionary decree ordering the suppression of religious communities was signed, monks at Jumièges numbered no more than eighteen. From 3 May, a municipal delegation arrived to proceed with an inventory of moveable property. The abbatial dwelling was put up for sale in 1791. As for the monastery premises, they served during two years as a retirement home for the friars of the suppressed establishments, then became barracks. In 1795, the ensemble was sold off as national heritage. The first buyer was a certain Sire Lescuyer, property manager, who rapidly effectuated building demolitions. After 1802, Jean-Baptiste Lefort, a lumber merchant at Canteleu, tackled the Church of Notre-Dame, where he knocked down a large part of the choir by utilising gunpowder to blow up the transept. Systematic demolitions ceased in 1824, when the property fell to Casimir Caumont, Lefort's son-in-law. Numerous elements nonetheless continued to be dispersed: between 1825 and 1835, a lot of sculpted stone was purchased by Lord Stuart of Rothesay, English ambassador in Paris, to decorate his Highcliffe Manor in Hampshire.

Stroller in the nave of Saint-Pierre, lithograph after a drawing by Vauzelle, in Taylor and Nodier's *Voyages pittoresques ...*, 1820 (Paris, BnF).

It was necessary to wait until 1853, date of the repurchase of the estate by Aimé Lepel-Cointet, Parisian stockbroker, in order for the ruins to be saved definitively. The Lepel-Cointet family instigated the last modifications to the domain. After acquiring the ruins and gateway, Aimé Lepel-Cointet had a Neo-Gothic building added to the latter. The ground floor (now occupied by the reception and a bookshop) and first-floor salon were fitted out as a museum to present sculptural elements which derived from the abbatial buildings. Lepel-Cointet's son-in-law next bought the former abbot's dwelling, separated from the abbey's buildings, which permitted reconstitution of the 18th-century property by reuniting the two estates.

Bust of Madame Lepel-Cointet (Collection de l'abbaye).

Classified in two phases, 1918 and 1947, the ensemble was bought by the State in 1946. Today the domain enjoys a new existence, oriented toward the evocation of a past whose spiritual dimension is forever present, and linked to a kind of romanticism which emanates from the juxtaposition of stone and nature.

The *voyage pittoresque*

Aware of the exceptional interest of the site for the history of both medieval art and architecture, archaeologist Auguste Le Prévost and draughtsman Eustache Hyacinthe Langlois were amongst the first (from before 1820) to attract the attention of the intellectual world to the Jumièges ruins. Pages that Baron Taylor and Charles Nodier consecrated to them in their *Voyages pittoresques et romantiques dans l'ancienne France* in 1820, and then the visit of the Duchess of Berry in 1824 made them into a fashionable tourist attraction, becoming the obligatory pilgrimage of "antiquarians", writers and artists of the period.

Jumièges around 1832, Joseph Turner watercolour (London, Tate Gallery).

Neo-Gothic pavilion of the Lepel-Cointet family, with **lapidary museum** installed on the ground floor and **first-floor salon**, old post cards (Rouen, ADSM, and Collection de l'abbaye).

Ruins of the abbey circa 1830, anonymous oil on canvas (Villequier, Musée Victor-Hugo).

— 1835

…ant de chez l'immonde

…de Saint Wandrille.

…isite M. Casimir

…de avoir Jumièges

…ges de avoir M

…aumont. Visit

Victor Hugo.

…s curieux d'admirer les belles

…es ont parcourues aujourd'hui

14 août 1835

…Mélanie [illegible]

…cuyer fils

The Church of Notre-Dame

West façade

Likely raised around 1060, the present corps of the façade replaced the small Church of Saint-Sauveur, itself installed by Abbot Thierry († 1027) in the ancient tower of the Carolingian church. Such antecedents might help to explain the archaic aspect of the work, close to that of the "Western pillars" of Germanian churches circa 1000: a projecting galilee or porch housing a tribune on the first storey, with two large staircase towers on either side.
The unified design is impressive in its majesty and austere simplicity. Save for the presence of two great arches at their base whose function remains enigmatic, the quadrangular-planned towers present a smooth stack 28 metres high. Above, the wall is animated: two storeys decorated with arcatures, then two octagonal levels of unequal height. These latter complex structures, arranged in a contrasting manner, testify to the initial research of Norman architects into the domain of mural plasticity.

West tribune

In the church, on turning back, one sees the location of a tribune over the porch. Covered by a barrel vault♦ (redone in the 18th century), it opens onto the nave through a semicircular arch♦; originally the lower portion was protected by a balustrade formed by an open-work stone arcature.
One reaches this tribune by two staircases mounting in the thickness of the towers from the side aisles♦.
Its primary function—a chapel meant to protect the dais for the cantors—has yet to be elucidated.

Following double page
Aerial view, taken from the east, showing eroded vestiges of Notre-Dame's choir.

♦Barrel vault: *half-cylindrical vault.*

♦Semicircular arch: *circular or perfect arch.*

♦Side aisles: *lateral naves.*

Nave

With its 25-metre elevation, this is the loftiest Romanesque nave in Normandy. It is comprised of eight bays demarcated alternatively by cylindrical columns ("weak piers") and wide-sectioned masonry pillars ("strong piers"). The reason for this alternance has been amply discussed. Today one favours the hypothesis of the presence of transversal arches, at the level of the strong piers intended to guarantee the connection between the two nave walls. Whatever the explanation, it is certain that originally this nave had only a wood ceiling. Between 1688 and 1692, it was replaced by a false plaster vault resting on consoles whose location was mended at the holes which early 19th-century demolishers had left in extracting them. The walls which frame the nave are made up of three storeys: the ground floor with great arcades, the intermediate with bays opening onto the tribunes above the side aisles, and uppermost clerestory with a row of windows.

The capitals of the large arcades end at some slightly rough-hewn cubes, with the outline of volutes at the angles. They might have supported a painted decor, now vanished. Only the north side aisle conserves its original roof covering: a groin vault♦ compartmentalised by transverse arches♦. The tribunes situated above might possibly have had vaults of this same type.

♦**Groin vault:** *vault whose compartments are joined to form squared edges, without ribs to support them.*

♦**Transverse arch:** *banded main arch under a vault.*

Transept

Of the great tower which rose from the transept crossing, there survives only the west wall with its staircase turret suspended from the north corner. At the summit, two rows of openings are visible. Those at the top correspond to the storey of the bells, those below to windows which illuminated the centre of the crossing, from hence derives the term "lantern towers" for constructions of this sort. Although heavily modified at the end of the 12th and beginning of the 13th centuries, the transept conserves its original volume. Each cross bar♦ is covered with a tribune, a platform destined for a group of cantors. On the first storey, one notices a narrow circulation gallery fitted into the wall thickness. Together with Notre-Dame de Bernay's (circa 1050), this is the oldest example of gangways♦ characteristic of Norman Romanesque churches.

♦**Cross bar:** *transept arm.*
♦**Gangway:** *circulation gallery fitted into a wall thickness.*

“During two nights, it is said, through fine moonlight,
A pale lady once appeared in this spot.”
Verse composed by Casimir Caumont on the occasion of Boieldieu’s visit to Jumièges on 16 October 1829.

Notre-Dame's 11th-century sculpted decoration

Detail of decorative interlacing.

Differing from nave capitals decorated only with paintings —a single case, at the far eastern end of the north side-aisle, conserves a few traces of original decoration—most choir and crossing capitals were sculpted. In the lapidary collection, eight Notre-Dame sculpted capitals are preserved. The most voluminous three, which are ornamented with a human figure, likely come from the transept tribune supports. The sculpted decor of Notre-Dame divides into two iconographic groups: capitals with plant-inspired motifs (comparable to ornamental borders in the school of Winchester's manuscripts) and capitals with figures or animals evoking Germanic art of around 1000, and probably inspired, too, by illuminated manuscripts.

Situated at the left cross bar entry, this celebrated capital shows a bird held in a medallion of encircling plant-like foliage. Again presenting parallels with those depicted in Anglo-Saxon illuminations, the decor was possibly modelled after an English manuscript donated by Robert Champart to the abbey in 1045.

Right and opposite page **Capitals with patterns of animals and vegetation.**

(Except where indicated, lapidary elements presented belong to the Jumièges Abbey deposit.)

Gothic choir

Despite archaeological surveys effectuated in 1927, incertitude remains over the Romanesque choir plan. All that now remains in this east portion results from a 1267-1278 reconstruction.
This large construction campaign comprised of installing seven radiating chapels around an ambulatory. The sole intact chapel is the second in the south ambulatory. The one contiguous, toward the transept, has lost its pointed vault♦ but retains its west wall. All the chapels had a single bay and square plan, except the one on axis with the apse♦: it consisted of a supplementary bay terminating with a cant♦. Rediscovered in the demolition rubbish, a large keystone with a Paschal lamb likely belongs in the ambulatory, an idea suggested by the radiating arrangement of ribs originating around the central medallion. Between choir and nave stands an ornate rood-screen♦ with low reliefs illustrating the passion of Christ; a crucifix is mounted above the ensemble. Two retable fragments representing scenes of the Annunciation and the Visitation could come from nowhere else except the Church of Notre-Dame. Very finely executed, they embellished either the main altar consecrated in 1278, or the slightly later north altar of the chapel of the Virgin. Under a black-marble slab in the north transept chapel is buried the heart of Agnès Sorel, Charles VII's mistress, called the Dame de Beauté, deceased on 9 February 1450 in the Manoir de la Vigne, near Jumièges.

♦Pointed or Gothic vault: *vault resting on a ribbed crossing within pointed arches.*

♦Apse: *semicircular termination of a church, housing the choir and high altar.*

♦Cant or clipped gable: *a wall is said to be "canted" when its outline is polygonal.*

♦Rood-screen: *major transverse tribune erected between the nave and choir.*

Church of Notre-Dame Sculpted panels ornamented with scenes of the Visitation and Annunciation.

Opposite page **Vestiges of the ambulatory chapels** *(top).* **Keystone from the choir vault** *(bottom, left).* **Fragment from Agnès Sorel's tomb** *(bottom, right).*

Bas-relief, 15th-century showing a scene from the Passion, undoubtedly from the Church of Notre-Dame's rood-screen.

"Charles-VII arcade"

On leaving the south transept (where sacristy and vestibule are located), one joins up with the Church of Saint-Pierre through a covered arcade called the "Charles-VII arcade". Constructed in the early 1330s, it dates in fact over one century earlier than the king's reign. Through this passage the monks arrived each day to their monastic lodgings situated behind the Church of Saint-Pierre, or Notre-Dame, where most services took place.

The arcade was often used by processions occurring on fixed dates within different parts of the monastery.

The Church of Saint-Pierre

Gothic sections

By the 13th century, the Church of Saint-Pierre was so dilapidated that it was believed to date from the time of Saint Philibert (7th century). Nave and choir were reconstructed in two phases: at the end of the 8th century, the south side with its side aisle and chapel of Saint-Martin were refitted; between 1332 and 1349, the north-side tower and choir. On the south side, the late 13th-century arcades opened onto a farmyard now vanished. The chapel of Saint-Martin retains

Arcades facing north; pedestals under the capitals served as supports for statues of an "apostolic cortege".

Saint-Martin chapel entry.

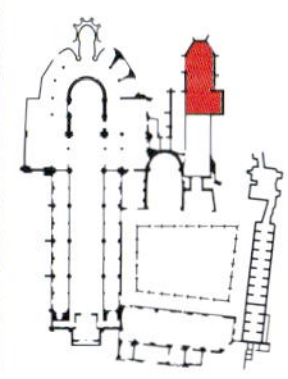

1
2

evidence of a very ancient oratory to the south of Saint-Pierre that, already in the 8th century, is mentioned in *La Vie de saint Philibert*. It is also through the recollection of layouts described in the Carolingian text that, at the end of the 13th century, above the chapel, one constructed "Saint Philibert's chamber", an evocation of the cell in which the abbey's founder had lived. Sculpted in the late 13th century, a **keystone**[3] from the chapel of Saint-Martin illustrates the legend of Saint Philibert and the wolf: after a wolf had slain a donkey delivering linen washed by nuns of Pavilly to the Jumièges monks, Philibert subdued the animal and succeeded in having the donkey replaced. The north-side Gothic arcades open onto a side aisle which communicates with the "Charles-VII arcade".
Rib-vaulted, the choir is reinforced by a series of counterforts♦ surmounted by pinnacles♦. Slightly after the choir and Gothic nave were terminated, their piers were decorated with great **statues representing the twelve apostles**[2-4]. Several amongst them were found at Duclair, where they had been transferred in 1791 to embellish the parish church. Installed in the Church of Saint-Pierre's choir, the double **tomb "des Énervés"**[1] was executed to receive two ancient sepulchres, found in the neighbouring chapel during the early 12th century. It is believed possible to identify these bodies as those of Tassilon of Bavaria and his son Theodon, whose sejourn and death in Jumièges at the time of Charlemagne is evoked in a 10th-century legend. The name "tombeau des Énervés" results in the link (no doubt erroneous) to another legendary story, that of Queen Bathilde's two sons who, punished for revolting, had their leg nerves severed. Abandoned adrift in a boat on the Seine, they landed up at Jumièges.

♦*Counterfort:* *masonry pier intended to buttress a wall or to receive lateral thrusts from a flying buttress.*

♦*Pinnacle:* *in Gothic buildings, the stone spire surmounting a counterfort.*

4

Vestiges of the Carolingian nave, seen from the south-east.

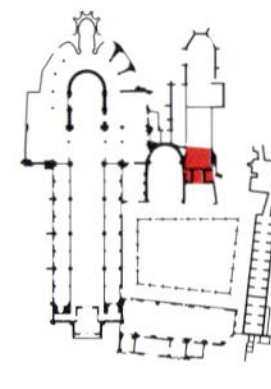

The Carolingian sections

The dating of these masonry wall sections has been passionately debated by archaeologists.
The most recent analyses appear to situate their construction in the opening decades of the 9th century. Sole vestiges at Jumièges predating the Viking raids, they also constitute the most important Carolingian monument still standing in northern France, according to present knowledge. Two double-heighted bays survive from the original nave. The lower one is occupied by two great arcades which once opened on to the side aisles, since disappeared, and in which were fitted some chapels during the 10th-century restoration. The north chapel, destroyed in the late 11th century to accomodate the chapter house, was dedicated to Saint Clement, that of the south to the Saints Innocent. Above the great arcades, the walls were embellished with convave medallions. In the 19th century, traces of painted figures in the Byzantine style were still visible there, among them the bust of a queen or empress holding a terrestrial globe. These paintings perhaps date back to the 10th-century restoration campaign. On the upper floor, the twin bays illuminated the tribunes installed above the side aisles. To the west the church was preceded by a vaulted porch, framed by two quadrangular turrets which housed staircases permitting access to a tribune situated above the porch, opening onto the tower through a large bay. From one end to the other of this opening (now walled up)—note remains of painted decoration on

Traces of painted decoration on the arch of the tribune.

Two Carolingian capitals from Saint-Pierre (Collection de l'abbaye).

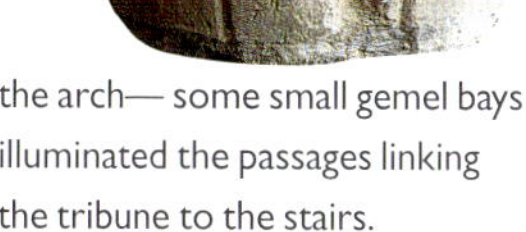

the arch— some small gemel bays illuminated the passages linking the tribune to the stairs. Decorated with plant-like motifs of great variety, the capitals surmounting the tower's first-floor bay colonnettes are the only capitals from the Carolingian epoque now known in Normandy. In Caen stone, they undoubtedly came from a workshop in Bessin, an important production centre of early 9th-century sculpted decor.

Tribune gemel bays of the transept north arm.

Masonry pier of the staircase turrets, west view.

The cloister demarcated by the Churches of Notre-Dame and Saint-Pierre, detail from the Delavigne plan, 1674 (Paris, Archives nationales).

Monastery buildings

Cloister

The cloister constituted the heart of the abbey and was used for promenades and meditation, as well as work. There, 11th-century copyists often set up their pulpits. On regular occasions, it was animated by processions and ceremonies, such as the washing of feet on Holy Thursday. Only a single empty space remains with a yew tree in the centre.

A 17th-century drawing depicts a quadrilateral of galleries covered with a sloping roof, surrounding a courtyard decorated with parterres.

To the left is the Church of Notre-Dame, to the right the refectory, in the distance Saint Peter, and in the foreground, the former hostelry turned storeroom. Of the cloister architecture, we know only about the most recent state, concerning a reconstruction during the 1530s under Abbot François de Fontenay. The galleries were then covered with vaults following a refined and complex design: each compartment was fashioned as a four-pointed star with four diamond-shaped pendant keystones.

At its tip, each keystone held an openwork ornament in the form of a lantern. Each bay, in Flamboyant style, was divided into three by thin ribs. Under the cloister galleries, walls were embellished with frescoes illustrating the legends of the "Énervés", Saint Aycadre, Jumièges' conflagration by the Vikings, the encounter between Guillaume Longue-Épée and the two brothers Baudoin and Gandoin.

Cloister keystone, 16th century (Collection de l'abbaye).

Chapter house

Each morning a chapter from the rules of Saint Benedict was read in this hall. Internal monastic affairs were also debated here. Monks were seated on benches along the walls; the abbot, seated in the back within the apse. Its extension having been restricted at the rear by a passage linking Saint-Pierre to Notre-Dame, the building was given great width, unusual for a Romanesque chapter house.
Its construction extended back to the late 11th or early 12th century. It was covered with an intersecting ribbed vault which is, with that of the abbey church of Lessay (Manche region), one of the oldest examples of this type of Norman roofing. Originally the apse received light from three bays framed by colonnettes surmounted by plant-decorated capitals. At the end of the Middle Ages, these openings were replaced by two rectangular windows.

By the early 12th century and for one and one-half centuries, the chapter house was the site where abbots were buried: this tradition has retained the memory of twelve sepulchres disposed in rows. The most ancient is that of Abbot Urson († 1127), who probably had the hall built. In the 13th century, these tombs were indicated by sumptuously enamelled terra-cotta flagging of which watercolour measured drawings have been preserved. Caumont stone sarcophagi built between the hall walls were installed in the 19th century.
The majority belonged to 12th-century abbey sepulchres. Research has also permitted the discovery of several abbatial crosiers, leather debris, and fabric.

Two sarcophagi discovered during excavations of the chapter house, 12th-13th century.

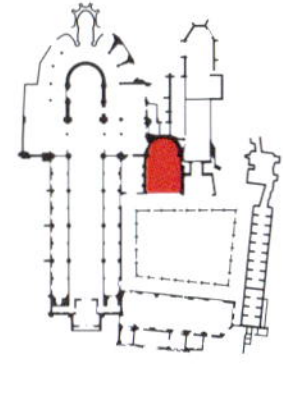

Wall arcade of the chapter house.

Treasury room

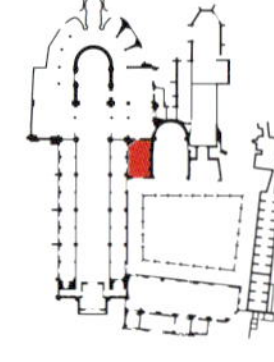

According to tradition, it was in these premises close to the transept of Notre-Dame that the treasury was kept. Constructed in the 12th century, this hall was covered with a barrel vault. The basic collection was made up of gold- and silver-plated shrines, reliquaries and precious book-bindings. Amongst the most remarkable pieces figure the shrines of Saints Aycadre, Valentin, Constantin and Pérégrin. Several times pillaged, dispersed or melted down, the Jumièges treasury included only a few objects of little value on the eve of the Revolution.

Vestiges of the serving hatch.

Hostelry

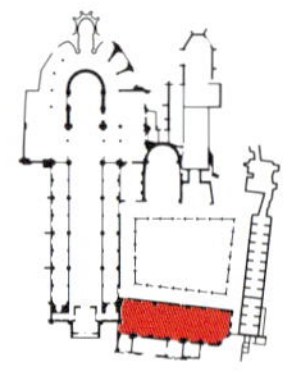

This grand 12th-century vaulted hall with impressive dimensions —a nave length of more than 35 metres, divided into seven bays— was originally destined to welcome distinguished guests to the abbey. During one or two centuries, numerous grand personages, kings, barons, and high church dignitaries were received with honours due their rank. Afterwards, the monks' relationship to the outside world having altered, the reception area was reduced to the north part of the building, closer to the Church of Notre-Dame. A 14th-century text indicates that, in the south section, a tailor's workshop was installed. The hostelry having been transferred from before the 15th century to the south of the cloister, the hall was converted to a storeroom. In 1665, the Maurists raised it by one storey to install a new library there. At the extreme north of the hall, a door (now sealed) allowed guests to arrive in the Church of Notre-Dame without mingling with the monks. From the mid-13th century, estimating that too many seculars were entering the monastic sites, the archbishops of Rouen demanded that the diocese abbots survey access to the cloisters more strictly; it might have been at this period that the door was blocked up. Conserved in its 12th-century condition, a small opening communicating with the kitchen was used as a serving hatch. It testifies to the first function of the hostelry: to honour high-ranking visitors, benefactors of

Hostelry great hall at the beginning of the 19th century, Eustache Hyacinthe Langlois drawing (Rouen, ADSM), and how it looks today.

West portal of the hostelry at the beginning of the 19th century, J. S. Cotman engraving.

the abbey, with grand receptions. Included in the little projecting pavilion, the original hostelry entry (now in ruin) was located to the west on axis with the monastery gateway. An engraving (1818) by J. S. Cotman serves as reminder of the rich Romanesque decoration with geometric motifs remaining on this guest door prior to its transfer to Highcliffe Castle in England around 1830. Raised in the first decades of the 12th century, the west façade wall

Wall decor, west façade, 12th century.

Modillion: *projecting stone, generally sculpted, supporting a cornice at the base of a roof.*

West portal, present state.

is the oldest part of the hostelry. Its sculpted decor offers a lively contrast to the plain walls of the neighbouring Church of Notre-Dame. In this building reserved for guests and secular visitors, the builders could give themselves over unrestrainedly to their decorative imagination—windows embellished with zigzag friezes, trefoiled arches, and bearded heads, a cornice with modillions♦ peopled with grotesque figures. At the extreme north-west of the ensemble are visible the ruins of a small premises, undoubtedly the guest-hall vestibule after the 14th century. The presence of stone banquettes designate this reduit as a "parlour", a place outside the enclosure where visitors could converse with the brothers without disturbing the tranquillity of the monastic sites. Some traces of the original hostelry roof are still apparent on the wall of the Church of Notre-Dame. In place of the loft, the Maurists raised a supplementary storey in 1665 to install their new library there. Sumptuously decorated, this vast work room quickly gained celebrity across the entire province, notably for the importance of its philosophy collection. On the eve of the Revolution, it housed more than 5,400 printed works and 392 manuscripts.

Vestibule-parlour, north-west corner.

Ruins of a cellar.

Houses built against the hostelry

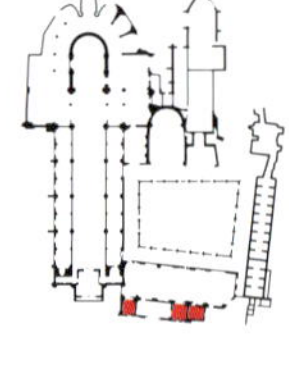

Running along the hostelry's central vestibule, ruins of two small dwellings leaning against the 12th-century building façade are visible.
They clearly have been modified and undoubtedly date much earlier than 1674, year of the Delavigne plan, the oldest to indicate their presence (Paris, Archives nationales).
Both contain a lower room for kitchen and storage with bedchambers on the upper floor (the grate of a chimneypiece is noticeable on the north dwelling's first floor).
These houses might have belonged to two "officers" of the abbey: responsible for worldly affairs, these secular administrators generally enjoyed rights to individual dwellings, removed from the monastic sites.

Refectory bay

A large Caen stone bay, covered by a basket-handle arch•, is all that remains of the refectory annex, a vast edifice that bordered the south cloister wing. Only rare details survive on the history of this building before 1770, the year in which the monks developed a project, rapidly abandoned, to transform it into a hostelry and infirmary. Without doubt the community had long ago deserted the medieval great hall to take their meals in the small, better heated "winter refectory".

Vestiges of the western gable of the refectory annex.

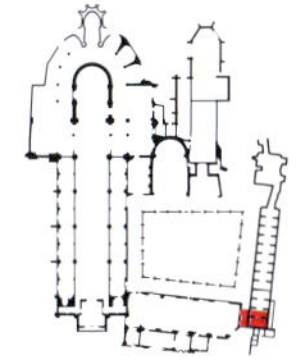

Basements and cellars
(exclusive of the visit)

For the convenience of the church service, cellars where the community stocked wine and food were located under the refectory annex, close to the kitchens. A narrow stair descending from the building's west gable gave access to a double series of thirteen small vaulted cellars aligned from one end to the other to a central aisle. Constructed in the 14th century, this gallery with lateral niches is a fine architectural example of Norman medieval cellars. To the south-east of the Church of Saint-Pierre, under the garden terrace, an imposing late 13th- or early 14th-century cellar, covered by four rib-vaulted bays resting on wide cylindrical pillars, formed the basement of the first abbatial dwelling, reconstructed by Abbot de Martimbos from 1607 to 1613. Several 17th-century views restitute the silhouette of this tall, two-storeyed pavilion, coiffed with a voluminous full-hipped roof. From the abbatial dwelling basement begins a narrow subterranean gallery passing along the length of the Church of Saint-Pierre, under the dormitory site which Abbot Philippe de Luxembourg had constructed from 1516 for the first reform monks. The south extremity of this tunnel opens out onto a handsome 17th-century vaulted cellar.

Left page, bottom
Basement of the first abbatial dwelling, under the garden, old postcard (Collection de l'abbaye).

•Basket-handle arch: *flat arch with a radius lower than that of a semicircular arch.*

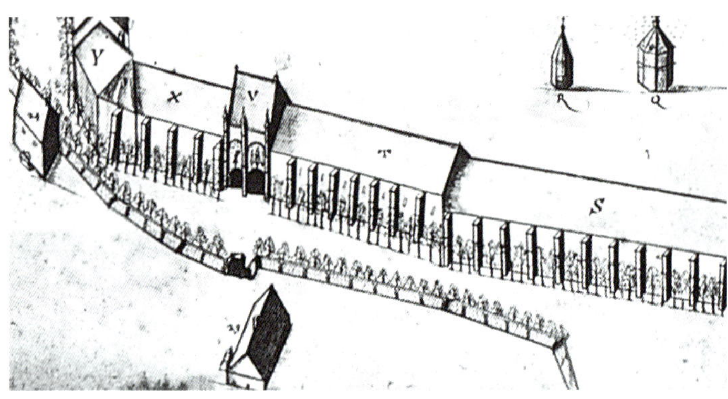

Former gateway renovated in the 19th century, east view.

Gateway abbey reception buildings in 1674, detail of the Delavigne plan (Paris, Archives nationales).

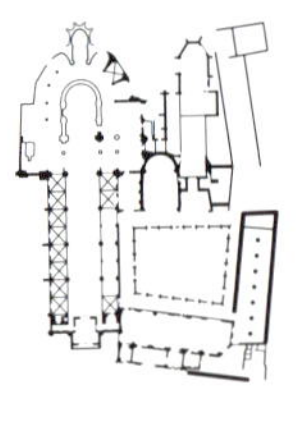

The gateway

Situated on axis with the hostelry door and the Church of Saint-Pierre, the abbatial entry pavilion has undoubtedly occupied its site since ancient times. Constructed in the mid-14th century, the church porch itself is covered with four ribbed vaults resting on a central octagonal pillar. According to custom, access from the street was made through two bracketed portals of unequal dimensions, the higher to the south for the passage of wagons, the lower to the north for pedestrians. The visitor was welcomed by statues of the monastery's patron saints fixed to the façade wall.

On the reverse side of the building, a staircase put into a pentagonal hipped roof tourette led into a hall situated above the entry. This was the "praetorium" where legal audiences of the abbey were held. From one end of the gateway to the other, leaning against the enclosure wall, two vast buildings housed the stables and one of the most important and ancient offices of the abbey (attested from the 9th century), that of the chaplaincy: there, every day, clothes and nourishment were distributed to the needy. Under the Second Empire, the abbey proprietors transformed the southern annex

Porch interior of the gateway, 14th century, and detail of a keystone.

of the old hostelry into a Neo-Gothic pavilion, a fine example of the taste for medieval and Renaissance decors, "Gothic Revival" having become fashionable in England from the 1780s. One notices on the exterior several patterns inspired very freely from buildings of the Middle Ages (gargoyles, escutcheons with the abbey arms, fenestration, and the like). Under restoration, the interior decoration has retained the handsome coffered ceilings, together with Flamboyant and trompe-l'oeil woodwork elements.

Abbatial dwelling and park

***Mansard roof:** hipped-gable or gambrel roof housing an habitable storey.*

The building was installed at the summit of a hill (where now a beautiful view on the ruins of Notre-Dame is afforded), constructed between 1666 and 1671 by Abbot François de Harlay de Champvallon. This imposing edifice is a veritable castle with mansard roof♦ pierced with dormers and two floors of bays framing a slightly projecting pavilion. Its terrace gives onto a formal garden; to the rear are found vast outbuildings, remaining very close to their original state. At the end of the 17th century, if one excludes the garden of the abbatial dwelling at the end of an enclosure, the abbey park is comprised of three parts, separated by long walls covered in espaliers: an orchard behind the Church of Notre-Dame (qualified as the "new garden" in 1674); a garden divided into parterres "*à la française*" on three levels of terraces to the south and east of the Church of Saint-Pierre; and a great park traversed by avenues planted to the south of the ensemble. Reverted to meadows and shaded by copses, these spaces now permit agreeable promenades with splendid views of the ruins.

***Double-helix staircase:** staircase made up of levels of semicircular ramps.*

The terraces of the central garden have survived, as has an imposing double-helix staircase♦ to the south of Saint-Pierre's chevet.
Further south, an allée leads to

a small crest crowned with trees: this is the "Thabor", a hill arranged by the monks in the 17th century to evoke Mount Thabor in Judea where tradition situates the transfiguration of Christ.
A double range of trees preserves the memory of an avenue traced in the 17th century to link the abbey outbuildings with a little service door pierced into the south portion of the enclosure wall.
The 19th-century contribution involved "making acceptable" the ruined status of the buildings, by favouring the romantic atmosphere evoked by their devastations. Many trees were planted. Certain of them are now superb: two great purple beeches (one is spotted to the left in ascending toward the abbatial dwelling), two pines in front of the gateway, a few maple sycamores, some hornbeams. Below the abbatial dwelling, a *broderie de buis* [interweaving pattern of boxwood beds] was redesigned a few years ago in the spirit of the one created in the 1900s by the celebrated landscapist Achille Duchêne.

A short bibliography

Baylé, Maylis, "La sculpture du XIe siècle à Jumièges et sa place dans le décor architectural des abbayes normandes", *Aspects du monachisme en Normandie (IV-XVIIIe siècle)*, edited by Lucien Musset, Paris, Vrin, 1982, 75-90.

Ibid., "Les origines et les premiers développements de la sculpture romane en Normandie", *Arts de la Basse-Normandie*, n° 100 *bis*, n.d.

Decaens, Henri, and **Champollion, Hervé,** *Jumièges*, Paris, CNMHS/Ouest-France, 1996.

Jumièges Congrès scientifique du XIIIe centenaire, collective work, Rouen, 1955, 2 vols.

Martin du Gard, Roger, *L'Abbaye de Jumièges...*, Montdidier, Impr. Grou-Radenez, 1909.

Musset, Lucien, *Normandie romane*, vol.II, *La Haute-Normandie*, La Pierre-qui-Vire, "Zodiaque" collection, 1974.

Taralon, Jean, *Jumièges*, Paris, 1955.

ADMS: Archives départementales de Seine-Maritime, Rouen.

BM: Bibliothèques municipales, Rouen.

BnF: Bibliothèque nationale de France, Paris.

CMN: Centre des monuments nationaux, Paris.

MDSM: Musées départementaux de Seine-Maritime, Rouen.

Captions

Cover
Front: Church of Notre-Dame, transept crossing.
Back: hostelry, west façade decor.
Front flap: chapter house bay.
Back flap:
Church of Notre-Dame nave.
Visit, p. 34:
Victor Hugo's signature in Jumièges' golden book (ADSM), 1835.

Chronology
From left to right and from top to bottom:
• Political life: William the Conqueror, Bayeux tapestry (Bayeux, Centre Guillaume-le-Conquérant), Médiathèque de l'architecture et du patrimoine, Archives photographiques; Saint-Louis, *Grandes Chroniques de France*, 13th c., Bibliothèque Sainte-Geneviève, Paris; Charles VII (p. 22), RMN, Paris; Napoleon and the French Revolution, Paul Chenavard's project for the Pantheon, 1848 (Lyon, Musée des Beaux-Arts), CMN/C. Rose.
• Religious life: Abbey Saint-Georges de Boscherville, draughted by Besnard, 1895 (Médiathèque de l'architecture et du patrimoine, Archives photographiques, Paris), CMN/P. Léger; Abbey de Saint-Wandrille, engraving from *Voyages pittoresques...*, Taylor and Nodier, 1820, CMN/Ph. Berthé.
• Jumièges Abbey: Queen Bathilde's tunic (p. 4), Musée municipal, Chelles; ornamented letter (p. 11), BM, Rouen; Church of Notre-Dame model (p. 15), CMN/D. Bordes; hostelry façade (p. 56), CMN/D. Bordes; Church of Saint-Pierre (p. 47), CMN/C. Rose; abbatial dwelling (p. 62), CMN/D. Bordes; Church of Saint-Pierre in ruins, Inventaire général de Haute-Normandie/ADAGP/ Y. Miossec/BnF; Musée lapidaire (p. 31), Collection de l'abbaye; abbot's crosier from Jumièges, 12th c. (Rouen, Musée départemental des Antiquités), Rouen, MDSM.

Photographic credits

Agence Giraudon, Paris: 23; AKG, Paris: 7; BnF, Paris: 2-3, 5t,8t, 9, 26b, 28; BM, Rouen: 11, 12, 13t, 14b, 15b, 16-17; CMN/B. Acloque: cover, 1c; CMN/Ph. Berthé: 20-21, 31, 34, 59t; CMN/D. Bordes: front flap, back cover, 1b, 13b, 15c, 22b, 26t, 30t, 35b, 39t, 42t, 43, 44c and b, 45, 46, 47b, 48, 49, 50, 51, 52b, 53, 54, 55b, 56b, 57, 58, 59, 60, 61, 62t; CMN/ Ch. Boulanger: inside front flap, 36-37; CMN/C. Rose: 38, 44t, 47t; CMN/O. Verley: back flap, 1t, 35t, 40-41, 42b, 62b, 63; Collection de l'abbaye: 31c and b; Collection du Parc de Brotonne: 19b; Inventaire général de Basse-Normandie/ Pascal Corbierre/ADAGP/ 1982/Bibliothèque municipale de Bayeux: 8b, 15t; Inventaire général de Haute-Normandie/ ADAGP/C. Kollman: 24-25, 56t/Y. Miossec: 28, 29, 52t, 55t, 61b; J. Le Maho: 5b, 19t and c; Musée départemental Victor-Hugo, Villequier/ Yohann Deslandes: 32-33; Musée municipal, Chelles: 4; MDSM, Rouen/Yohann Deslandes: 10, 18/François Dugue: 14t; Muséum d'histoire naturelle, Rouen: 21b; RMN, Paris: 22t; Tate Gallery, London: 30b; Olivier Verley: 27.

Collection director
Alix Sallé
Editorial coordinators
Clarisse Deniau
Alix Sallé
Documentation coordinator
Cécile Niesseron-Brenot
Translator
Barbara Shapiro Comte
Copy editor
Elizabeth Ayre
Graphic Design
Atalante/Paris
Layout
Stéphane Dallé-Asté
Graphics
Jean-Philippe Guillerme
Production coordinator
Carine Merse
Photoengraving
Scann'Ouest/ La Chapelle-sur-Erdre
Printing
Néotypo/ Besançon, France

Monum, Éditions du patrimoine, Paris, 2001

Dépôt légal: April 2001
Reprinting: August 2004